Catharsis

L.M.P.

Since I've lost you,
I have decided to lose everything else in my
life.
This is my best attempt to tell my journey.

Preface

So losing Kristina really shattered me. Like in all meaning of the word. I truly don't believe in divorce and yet it happened. I failed her, I failed my marriage, I failed myself most of all. To be honest I still haven't fully recovered and I'll probably never be the same. I have spent years now trying to figure what happened with so many things as well as trying to salvage my life to have resemble something to call my own.

Alas all have been in vain. I have been asking the wrong questions as well as seeking answers in the wrong places. It will never make sense nor will it ever be possible to explain; but to regain control of my world I must first surrender to it. To become stronger I must understand my weakness. To become wise I must become lost. To seek courage I must first know my greatest fears.

Those are key when it comes to bettering my world. Before I can continue though I have to surrender. For if you truly love, you must completely surrender to it.

Kristina may not see with her eyes what I do for her or how I speak of her, but maybe just maybe when she closes her eyes she can feel my love for her and hopefully in those times she needs it most my love will give her warmth to keep going.

They say before you traverse the darkness to take with you only thought that's strong enough to withstand the trails you will face. I took her. All of her. All the moments all the joy and all the sorrow. They didn't say what was the purpose of it. I thought it was so I would stay strong and endure. However no matter what you do, you lose everything in the abyss only to find it all over again, but never the same.

These are my collective thoughts, dreams, and musings since that fateful night I met my wife. Five years in the making.

Kristina, I am now talking to you, regardless how many read this book. This is solely for you. I hope this shines a light wherever you may need it.

Love,
Logan

Why I do it.

Waking up to you
is the only thing
that is keeping me alive.

Actions>Words.

I love you more than the words I have to
say.
Though I can use my most generous, most
beautiful
words I know to explain to you
how deep my love runs for you
I'd rather show you with a kiss.
Even if that be the last moment
I ever share with you.
I would rather show you my love
with an embrace over a word.

A Lovely Lyric 1.

A heart that is broken
makes a beautiful sound.
- Brandi Carlile

Effort.

I'd rather be the guy
who says too much
than not enough.

Ethereal Cognizance 1.

We just showered and
we were talking about
our honeymoon.
I could still feel your wet hair
touching my face and
how your neck felt as I kissed you.
Seeing your smirk in the mirror
each time I kissed you.
Then flashed to you in a blue dress
with red lips
and a beautiful necklace
Then I woke up.

A Perfect Person

I wish one day
to have a daughter
with your beauty
and my imagination
paired with our
shared intellect
and boundless capacity for love.

A Closer Look.

When I speak of my loss
all they see is
a marriage that failed
They don't see
the children
I will never see grow
The peace that
this woman brought
to my life
 now turned to ruin.

My worst reality

My greatest fear
is to find
what I'm looking
for in life
only
to destroy it.

What I really wanted to say in February.

Haven't found solid ground yet
I took a leap a faith
when it seemed faith was an impossible
feat.
Through my decent
I found myself lost in a cognitive dissonance
with agony and despair to guide me further
into the abyss.
I'm still falling and
I know I have quite a ways to go
but I am sure when God finds me ready
I will land with grace and clarity.

With You.

A perfect day
is
where it's cold out
the sun is warm
on what touches
Where you hear nothing
the world being
in
its natural state
wind gently blowing.
With you.

<u>La Belle et la Bête.</u>

Her voice
is the melody
that soothes
the savage beast
within.

A Devastating Act for Romance.

I kept us alive
the best way I know how
I made it tragic
and in that sadness you are immortal.

Timing isn't Everything.

Regardless of when you entered my life
to me
you were the first
and only.

Honor Bound

I know my duty
to the world
to family
and
I know my duty to you
Wherever you go
I will follow
I will guard
willingly
with my life.

A Lovely Lyric 2

She feeds my deadly soul
She talks right to my soul.
-Future Islands

Inner Dialogue 1.

"What do you need?"
The one thing I need most in this world
is also the one thing that
is my mortal weakness
The only thing that can
cure my insomnia
my madness
quell my rage
is the only thing
that can kill me
with just a gaze
"...and that is..?"
Her...

Ethereal Cognizance 2.

Kristina and I
just laying down
I feel her
her warmth
her pulse
her scent
all that she is
she was real once more
then I woke up.

A Lovely Lyric 3

Out of sight, out of mind
doesn't mean
you're not mine.
-The Xx

Ethereal Cognizance 3.

Today I had a dream
we were together
at Great Grandma's
I kissed you
and you told me to stop.
Almost like
we were just together
for appearances
It was heart breaking.
then I woke up.

One Thing.

If you can only do one thing
in this life
then let it be finding something
to die for
Whether it be a person
an ideal
or a belief
If you're willing to die for it
then that's a life worth living.

One Brave Soul.

I wish to find that person
who can stare into me
and accept it all
I want someone
I can go the distance with
To fight for and
someone who will fight endlessly for me as
well.
I need someone
to become more
than this mortal shell
I wish to be boundless
limitless
To become far beyond
the capacity that this life dictates
for once they stare into me
like the abyss
I will stare back into them.

A Lifetime in a Moment.

Remember the bear I gave you?
Do you remember the reaction you had?
I do
I remember telling myself
I could live in that moment forever
I also remember wanting to give
that kind of joy
to you
forever.

A Lovely Lyric 4

It's easy to
hate yourself
when all your love
is in someone else
- Little Green Cars

Hope: The Undying

If even for a moment
I still make your skip
jump
or do anything other than it's suppose to
There is hope.

Where there is Poison there is a Remedy

Maybe we'll meet again,
when we are slightly older
our minds less hectic
and I'll be right for you
you'll be right for me
But right now
I am chaos to your thoughts
and you are poison to my heart.
-Unknown

Pillow Talk

"Sweetest dreams"
remember that?
You told me that
every night
before we went to bed.

A Few of My Favorite things 1.

I always loved
watching her get ready for the day.
As I laid in our bed
I would have one eye open
just to admire her for all that she is.

Captivating.

When I look at her
the rest of the world
is out of focus.

Wandering mind.

Still waters run deep
Just imagine if there
was a way to use your brain to full potential
So many anomalies
so many different perceptions in this world
The capacity of just one human being
fascinates me
Just take a moment
to relive the unique experiences you've had
in this life.
Immaculate
Traumatizing
Mediocre
makes no difference
the simple fact that you lived in the
moment
and you are better person for it
is all that matters
What inspires you?

Break your heart until it opens
(Rumi)

Break
I know
you are hurting
but you must continue
I urge you to endure
Keep breaking
I feel the pain
it is overwhelming and tragic
you must break
to walk through this fire
is an act of rebellion
a sign of strength
a tribute to serenity
I promise
you are almost done
I know
how fatigued you are
the burden you carry
all the damage done
this is preparation for all that
you asked for
but first you have to break.

A Declaration

I dedicate
none of my achievements
to you
for you
are my one true goal
Everything that I do
Everything that I become
is only to better prepare myself
for the day
I fulfill my dream
and become your man.

My Intention

I intend to better myself
until the time comes
where your eyes match mine
your lips meet mine
I will better this world
so that your heart can find mine once again.

The Goddess of my Heart

Her beauty doesn't end with her
Every curve
Every contour
every gleam in a set of starry eyes
I see her
She resides in the heavenly scents
that are in this earthly realm
she takes shelter in my dreams
and dances just out of arms reach
She reminds me every night
that she is the beauty
I feel
when I see beauty
in the waking world.

A Few of My Favorite things 2.

I miss watching you getting brain freeze
cause you would always
say out loud
"put your tongue on the roof of your mouth"
you would do it every time
and my heart would swoon
at your goofiness.

A Few of My Favorite things 3.

If we were being playful
or I said something clever
you would put your tongue
out and down to the side of your mouth.
I became like a dog
for my tail would wag.

A Lovely Lyric 5

She looks like the moon
so close yet
so far away.
-Future Islands

A Few of My Favorite things 4.

when you would make funny faces
ALL the time
I love thinking of all the things
you do that genuinely make me smile
I live for those moments

<u>Wanted.</u>

You used to own things on our behalf.
Like when you tell us "our waterfall"
or when you would say Rainier is
"my mountain"
I felt like I belonged
when you would confirm those things
I felt validated.

Inescapable Entity

There's no walking away
from the type of woman you are.
Among all the things you gave me
I cherish all the color you brought in my life

A Gift from the Goddess

With you
I saw heaven
everyday.

Acceptance

When the hurt came
we went to our innate attributes
I did what I know best
 that was to search for answers
I went everywhere
on this world except
I failed to see what it did to our bond
I looked everywhere
and didn't bother to look within ourselves
My blindness tainted
my loyalty
and your faithfulness.

A Brilliant Mind 1.

I think of you in colors that do not exist.
-Jemma Silvert

Word to the Wise

If you decide to fall in love
fall for their soul
because good looks fade
Vigor weakens
the mind slips
hearts break
but the soul
is the made
of the things
that last forever.

What a Minute Looks Like

Her.
Rage
Love
Peace
Sorrow
Distractions
Pain
Imagination
Companionship
Depression
Art
Strength
Serenity
Her...

<u>A Brilliant Mind 2.</u>

I'll make up for all the years
I was supposed to be kissing you.
-Leo Christopher

Inner Dialogue 2.

"Out of all the names
all the words we have in our collective mind
you decide to call me A Beast named
Flawed!?
What about me is so flawed?
If anything you are the broken one."
Well we are Flawed
its a name that humanizes you.
I needed something to call you
after all this time you
have just been an entity
You are the man I wish to be
in some aspects
you are more me than you.

Perceptions of me from the outside

You're like a storm
From far away you're beautiful
and you draw people to you
Once you actually get to you though
You're an absolute mess
You have so many wars going on in your
mind
you charge through everything
Destroying everything that touches you
You do that because you don't think your
worth anything
So you throw everything at them at once
They try to stay.
They hold on because they know
at the end of the storm
you can just rebuild
Make things better
stronger
You do this to yourself though
I don't think you know
what kind of person you are
You're so smart
poetic
romantic
tragic
beautiful
You just need someone
to withstand this storm that you are
It doesn't mean you are destined to be
alone.
-A.C.

If you must know...

I fear you because I don't understand you
I also love you for the same reason.

A Brilliant Mind 3.

"Confront the dark parts of yourself,
and work to banish them with
illumination and forgiveness
Your willingness to wrestle
with your demons will cause your angels to
sing
Use the pain as fuel
as a reminder of your strength."
-August Wilson

Lamprocapnos Spectabilis.

All my pain
all my anger
turns to naught
when I see your face
when I hear your voice
My heart melts
A touch from you would cause me to fall to
pieces.

A Life Lost, A Debt Paid.

These aren't just words to me
These are the things I feel everyday
I have experienced a life I thought
was never possible for me
Since I've lost that
all the things in my life are meaningless
The joy I have felt
the passion
the sincerity
Nothin' else comes close
I know what I want with no idea how to
obtain it.

Icarus

To burn for someone is to melt in the
process.
-Unknown

Fruits of Labor.

Earn your meal.
Earn your sleep.
Earn your peace.

Manikin

In a world where
everyone wears masks
a man discovers
the meaning of life
by removing
his mask and seeing for the first time.

Mashel Falls

Just like that
feelings hit me like a train.
When she told me
she loved me
for the first time
I cannot remember anything so rewarding.

Ethereal Cognizance 3

We were walking on a bridge
in France
when I looked back
I saw us
you
me
our daughter
our infant son
our family
walking hand in hand
with Rocko as well.
When I looked beside me
I see we were walking alone.
When I looked forward I saw no one.
once I crossed the bridge
I was with you
and you welcomed me with
open arms just as we began on the bridge
then I woke up.

The Hunter

I constantly find myself
staring into the abyss
Knowing full well the abyss gazes into me
I tell it to do its worst
for my storm has yet to come
Every day I awake
I tell it over and over again
to come at me
For when my storm does rise
they will see my light and fear me worse
than any evil in the abyss.

The Clock is Priceless

I don't know
how much time
we have but I don't want
to spend one second looking back.

Move with Purpose

We drift through this life
wondering where we belong
longing to be wanted
desperately wishing to be believed in.
Yearning to just find at least one person
who understands us
We put our faith and our hearts
in those who make home
more than a state of mind
We lose sight from time to time
because such a simple thing
to belong
is more an ideal than an idea
for those who find that
well you must surrender yourself entirely
to the dream.
Only than can you find the light you were
born with
and shine.

Love

I have loved many
I have loved immensely
I have loved when it was easy
I loved when it seemed impossible
I have prayed in the name of love
I have even prayed to love
I have, however
never felt a love as pure and as powerful as
I have with you.

Lovesick

When you left
you took all my love
I have accumulated
through my life with you
That's how I know I gave you everything.

A Hunter's Curse

I volunteered to walk into the abyss
I have hunted these beasts
that dwell inside my soul far too long
To the point
where I find myself looking like the very
thing I wish to destroy
I know I have asked for a path full of
suffering
a path you never wished for me to take
but it is a path that must be taken if I am
ever to find you again.

The Hunter's Dream

I will sink deep
deep in this ocean of nothingness
I will empty my vessel
so that I may hear love whisper to me
I will close my eyes so that I may see what
is lost
I will feel everything so that I may feel what
cannot be seen
May my heart beat to the rhythm of yours
and after all this
after my inevitable destruction
may I shine in the abyss
as a beacon of hope and undying love.

When Faith is lost.

Love
even when
that seems like the hardest thing to do.

Lesson Learned

If you don't show
her your love
someone else will.

The Goddess Nike

Success
will come naturally
when it is ready
until then
Endure
Grow.

A Brilliant Mind 4.

It's the things we love the most that destroys us.
-Suzanne Collins

A Brilliant Mind 5

We are shaped and fashioned by what we love.
-Johann Wolfgang von Goethe

Love=Knowledge

With every love
comes a lesson
every lesson
brings one closer
to understanding
life.

A Brilliant Mind 6

When you are loved you can do anything in creation.
-Paulo Coelho

A Brilliant Mind 7

The one you love and the one who loves you
are never, ever the same person.
-Chuck Palahniuk

A Brilliant Mind 8

There is always some madness in love.
But there is also always some reason in
madness.
-Friedrich Nietzsche

A Lovely Lyric 6

I wish I found you sooner so I could of loved
you longer.
-Hymnal

Lady Luck

I was never
the luckiest
because I had your love
 I am the luckiest because
I will always have your love.

Just in Case

No matter
what you know
I still love you.

Galatians 5:22

The fruit of the Spirit is love, joy, peace,
patience, kindness, goodness, faithfulness,
gentleness and self-control
Against such things there is no law.

Define: Heartbroken

A man paints the sky
to represent his love
for a woman but she is too fascinated
with the rocks on the ground.

A Brilliant Mind 9

Love knows no limit to its endurance
no end to its trust
no fading of its hope
it can outlast anything
Love still stands when all else has fallen
-Blaise Pascal

Hole-y Heart

God made a spot in my heart that only you
can fill.

A Symbol of Serenity

Our love is like our waterfall.
Continuously flowing water over rocks
the water changes the rocks
smooths them down
It cuts grooves in them
but it takes time and in that time
love leaves a mark on our hearts

Destiny

When I am with you
I am with my destiny
When you live
I flourish.

Mars and Venus

You are my goddess
I am your warrior
I will fight for you
until my last breath
and when I enter
the after life
I will protect always.

The Last Laugh

I burn all my masks
so you can see
my scar filled face
smiling at you.

A Modest Request

I do not ask to
touch
see
hear
smell
or to taste
I simply ask to feel and understand.

50/50

You are the first person
that truly deserves
the title
my other half
because ever since you left
I only feel just that
...half.

Moniker(s)

Keeper of my love
Queen of my dreams
Goddess of my heart
At the end of the day it's all about her.

Eternal

I want to transcend with you
I want to reach new
unimaginable heights
I forsake all desires of the flesh for you
My body on this earth belongs to you
As God as my witness
I give you my heart
you and only you
That is my gift
Eternal.

Mine

You keep me grounded
while I sweep you off your feet
We are an immaculate team
Kristina
because I love you
I promise
to keep you safe and ensure
we are always moving forward
When you need someone
to encourage you
I will be there To cheer you on
When you fall I will catch you
When you long for someone to smile at
turn to me
Wherever you are I will follow.

Yours

Logan
I promise to be there through
all the happy times
as well as the sad
through times of sickness and in health
I promise to inspire you each and everyday
to be the best you can be and help you
reach all your goals all while by your side
I promise to love you unconditionally
with everything that I am
you are the love of my life
my soulmate
this adventure of ours is only the beginning
and we have the rest of our lives to see how
our story unfolds.

Afterword

You're a wandering spirit and that caused you to run away. It's not a bad thing. I embrace you, Kristina. I have always been inspired by your ability to follow your dreams. You follow through on everything. I can only imagine what you go through everyday, but I want you to know it is ok. You are going to shine if you haven't already seen your light.

I fight endlessly for you not because it's too late or I cannot let go. I fight for us because its what I believe in and I always have. We are destined for greatness I know its hard to see through the darkness but know I am here right beside you and I follow you to the darkest corners of the universe. I don't want to tell you that no one will ever love you like I will or anything of the sort.

I am sure people will come into your life, love you and elevate you, but I want to be your constant, I want to be the man of your dreams, the father of your children, the man who wakes up and captivates your heart everyday. I am your goddamn warrior of love and, for you, my goddess; I devote everything that I am to you. You have awakened something inside me that has laid dormant for some time. So, if nothing else, I thank you.

I know this has made me transform into the man I needed to be for you, my family and the world. you have nothing to lose and everything to gain. I am not asking you to leave anything behind, rather I ask the universe to let you find me again. Where ever you wander I'll be here to make a home.

www.ingramcontent.com/pod-product-compliance
Lightning Source LLC
Chambersburg PA
CBHW021936040426
42448CB00008B/1102